2023
CALENDAR
FOR WRITERS
Expanded Edition
MAD MOUNTAIN
PUBLISHING

THIS SPECIAL EXPANDED EDITION INCLUDES A COMPLETE

30 Day Writing Notebook

AND BONUS MONTHLY CALENDARS!

June 2022 - January 2024

ISBN 978 0 578 36077 5

Photo Credits:

Cover:
'seahorse dream' © grandfailure (boat/door) and © Jesser (seahorses) www.fotosearch.ie

Interior:
2022, 2023, 2024 © DmitryGuzhanin www.fotosearch.ie
'camellia' © rocich www.fotosearch.ie
'eagle' © Sybirko www.fotosearch.ie
'cats' © Sliplee www.fotosearch.ie
'fish' © Sybirko www.fotosearch.ie
'sun & moon' © ilasia www.fotosearch.ie
'dragon' © Vyusur www.fotosearch.ie

Other Photos and Illustrations public domain images courtesy of Adobe and Pixabay

Cover Design by Cadhla Logan
Original Interior Design by Kimberly Coleman,
Creator of the Bestselling ***Calendar For Writers*** *Series*

MAD MOUNTAIN
PUBLISHING

I've published my Calendar For Writers since 2016 and through the years the format has, in general, remained the same but the contents evolve based on feedback from writers who find these workbooks beneficial to their creativity. Adding my new ***30 Day Writing Notebook*** *is meant to expand options for writers wanting to explore how they can manage their writing time without interfering with the creativity of it.*

These are workbooks you will either love or hate. If you are a 'new' writer you may find yourself getting organized and starting to write more, better, sooner simply with using my books to schedule and plan ahead or scribble a note to explore later when you have more time; if you are a more experienced writer, you might find the notebooks constrictive or remedial when they are simply meant to 'be there' for you, to give you a single place to stash your thoughts and notes and snips and articles... I found due to my ADD I could never successfully use writing planners so structured as to their pages with Plot or Character or Writing Prompts... nothing ever fit what I felt I needed to be writing and that assured that then I would write absolutely nothing at all.

I needed the freedom to explore my scattered thoughts on narrow-lined pages I could title or not title as I wished. I could scribble a note or a lyric, a character name, an author I wanted to read later, things like this and be able to find them the next week. My workbooks save a lot of time for myself by collecting my sticky notes from the past months and making it easy to get them sorted --- I stash them now inside my workbook and then organize them in the back and see what starts to work... I've now several Bestsellers under my pen names. It is all in finding just what works for you and your creativity. Ignore the critics and social media writing experts who tout their books and streams as the one sure thing you must believe to be a successful writer. We all have to find our own way and what works for our own self and sanity.

There is a lot to be said in our tech age for presence and simple functionality. These oversized notebooks harken back to the past when teens wanted a 'slam book' to scribble in or a reliable and sturdy (and fairly stain-resistant) stack of bound pages to carry with them. I personally love having my notes, work-in-progress, and my daily schedule all together; this has tremendously improved my creativity with my ADD and limited time for writing in the first place.

Whatever you seek for your writing life I hope you find it....often it comes down to the type of paper and style of ink pen (and ink color and flow, of course!) for myself. That calms my ADD for a bit and I can get on with my writing.

Thanks for reading!

Kimberly Coleman
Designer and Creator of the *Original*
Bestselling ***Calendar For Writers*** Series

"Writers are a superior breed. No one else can face so much rejection and still thrive."
— Susie Smith

2022

January

Su	Mo	Tu	We	Th	Fr	Sa
						1
2	3	4	5	6	7	8
9	10	11	12	13	14	15
16	17	18	19	20	21	22
23	24	25	26	27	28	29
30	31					

February

Su	Mo	Tu	We	Th	Fr	Sa
		1	2	3	4	5
6	7	8	9	10	11	12
13	14	15	16	17	18	19
20	21	22	23	24	25	26
27	28					

March

Su	Mo	Tu	We	Th	Fr	Sa
		1	2	3	4	5
6	7	8	9	10	11	12
13	14	15	16	17	18	19
20	21	22	23	24	25	26
27	28	29	30	31		

April

Su	Mo	Tu	We	Th	Fr	Sa
					1	2
3	4	5	6	7	8	9
10	11	12	13	14	15	16
17	18	19	20	21	22	23
24	25	26	27	28	29	30

May

Su	Mo	Tu	We	Th	Fr	Sa
1	2	3	4	5	6	7
8	9	10	11	12	13	14
15	16	17	18	19	20	21
22	23	24	25	26	27	28
29	30	31				

June

Su	Mo	Tu	We	Th	Fr	Sa
			1	2	3	4
5	6	7	8	9	10	11
12	13	14	15	16	17	18
19	20	21	22	23	24	25
26	27	28	29	30		

July

Su	Mo	Tu	We	Th	Fr	Sa
					1	2
3	4	5	6	7	8	9
10	11	12	13	14	15	16
17	18	19	20	21	22	23
24	25	26	27	28	29	30
31						

August

Su	Mo	Tu	We	Th	Fr	Sa
	1	2	3	4	5	6
7	8	9	10	11	12	13
14	15	16	17	18	19	20
21	22	23	24	25	26	27
28	29	30	31			

September

Su	Mo	Tu	We	Th	Fr	Sa
				1	2	3
4	5	6	7	8	9	10
11	12	13	14	15	16	17
18	19	20	21	22	23	24
25	26	27	28	29	30	

October

Su	Mo	Tu	We	Th	Fr	Sa
						1
2	3	4	5	6	7	8
9	10	11	12	13	14	15
16	17	18	19	20	21	22
23	24	25	26	27	28	29
30	31					

November

Su	Mo	Tu	We	Th	Fr	Sa
		1	2	3	4	5
6	7	8	9	10	11	12
13	14	15	16	17	18	19
20	21	22	23	24	25	26
27	28	29	30			

December

Su	Mo	Tu	We	Th	Fr	Sa
				1	2	3
4	5	6	7	8	9	10
11	12	13	14	15	16	17
18	19	20	21	22	23	24
25	26	27	28	29	30	31

•
•
•
2
0
2
2

"So long as you write what you wish to write,
that is all that matters; and whether it matters for ages
or only for hours, nobody can say."
— Virginia Woolf

JUN2022

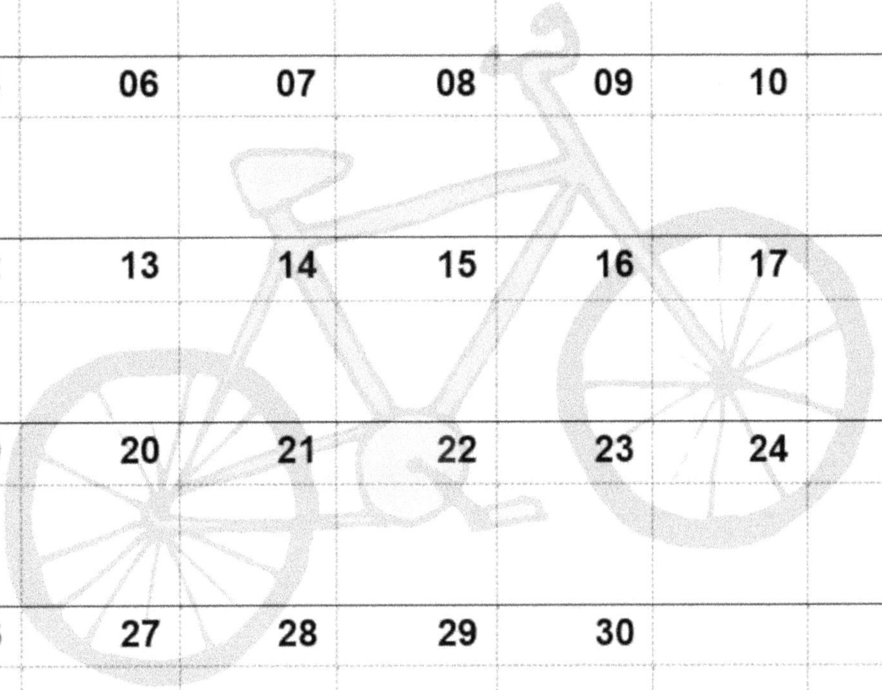

SUN	MON	TUE	WED	THU	FRI	SAT
			01	02	03	04
05	06	07	08	09	10	11
12	13	14	15	16	17	18
19	20	21	22	23	24	25
26	27	28	29	30		

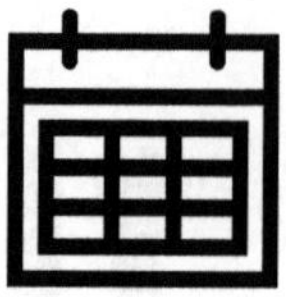

"Reading is the sole means by which we slip, involuntarily,
often helplessly, into another's skin, another's voice, another's soul."
— Joyce Carol Oates

JUL2022

SUN	MON	TUE	WED	THU	FRI	SAT
					01	02
03	04	05	06	07	08	09
10	11	12	13	14	15	16
17	18	19	20	21	22	23
24	25	26	27	28	29	30
31						

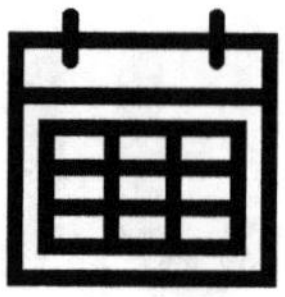

"What a blessing it is to love books as I love them: to be able to converse with the dead, and to live amidst the unreal!"
— Thomas Babington Macaulay

AUG2022

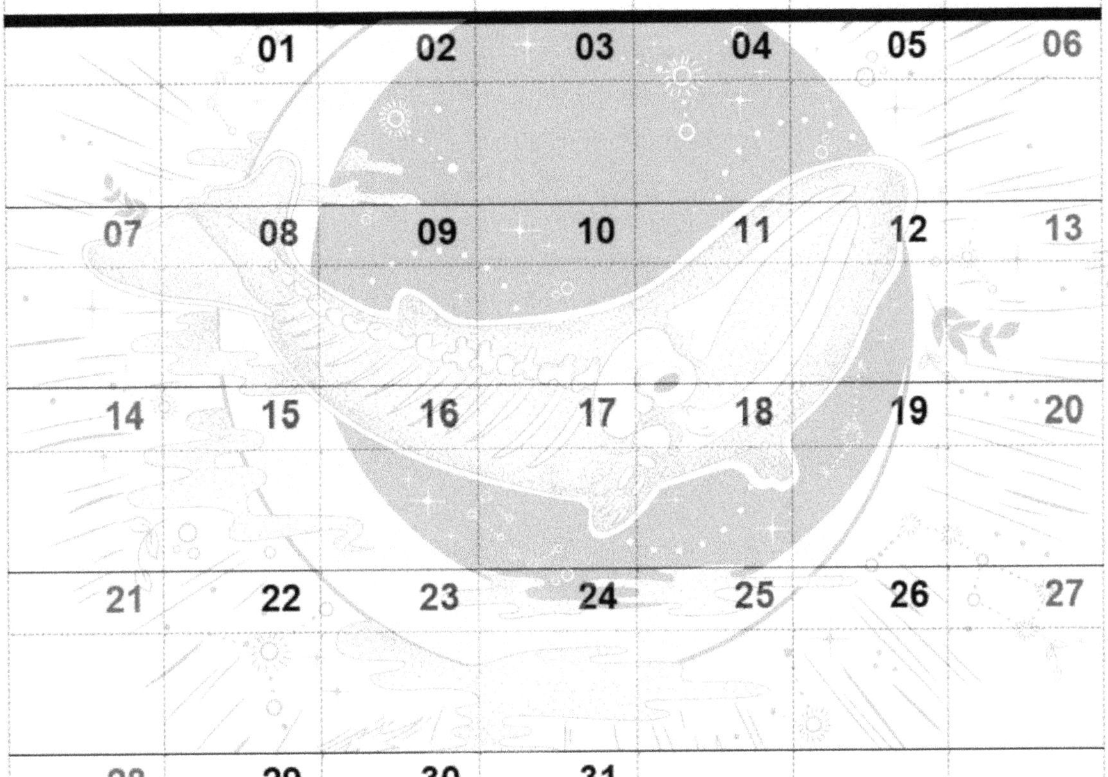

SUN	MON	TUE	WED	THU	FRI	SAT
	01	02	03	04	05	06
07	08	09	10	11	12	13
14	15	16	17	18	19	20
21	22	23	24	25	26	27
28	29	30	31			

"Good writing is remembering detail. Most people want to forget. Don't forget things that were painful or embarrassing or silly. Turn them into a story that tells the truth."
— Paula Danziger

SEP2022

SUN	MON	TUE	WED	THU	FRI	SAT
				01	02	03
04	05	06	07	08	09	10
11	12	13	14	15	16	17
18	19	20	21	22	23	24
25	26	27	28	29	30	

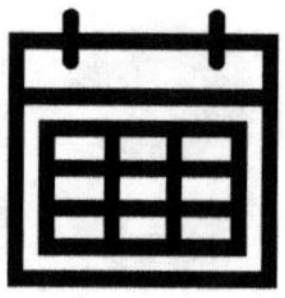

"Immature poets imitate; mature poets steal;
bad poets deface what they take, and good poets
make it into something better, or at least something different."
— T.S. Eliot

OCT2022

SUN	MON	TUE	WED	THU	FRI	SAT
						01
02	03	04	05	06	07	08
09	10	11	12	13	14	15
16	17	18	19	20	21	22
23	24	25	26	27	28	29
30	31					

*"The voice of the sea is seductive, never ceasing,
whispering, clamouring, murmuring, inviting the soul
to wander in abysses of solitude."*
— Kate Chopin

NOV2022

SUN	MON	TUE	WED	THU	FRI	SAT
		01	02	03	04	05
06	07	08	09	10	11	12
13	14	15	16	17	18	19
20	21	22	23	24	25	26
27	28	29	30			

*"My first feeling was that there was no way to continue.
Writing isn't like math; in math, two plus two always
equals four no matter what your mood is like.
With writing, the way you feel changes everything."
— Stephenie Meyer*

DEC2022

SUN	MON	TUE	WED	THU	FRI	SAT
				01	02	03
04	05	06	07	08	09	10
11	12	13	14	15	16	17
18	19	20	21	22	23	24
25	26	27	28	29	30	31

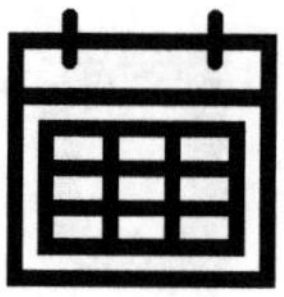

"It does not do to leave a live dragon out of your calculations, if you live near him."
— J.R.R. Tolkien

2023

January

Su	Mo	Tu	We	Th	Fr	Sa
1	2	3	4	5	6	7
8	9	10	11	12	13	14
15	16	17	18	19	20	21
22	23	24	25	26	27	28
29	30	31				

February

Su	Mo	Tu	We	Th	Fr	Sa
			1	2	3	4
5	6	7	8	9	10	11
12	13	14	15	16	17	18
19	20	21	22	23	24	25
26	27	28				

March

Su	Mo	Tu	We	Th	Fr	Sa
			1	2	3	4
5	6	7	8	9	10	11
12	13	14	15	16	17	18
19	20	21	22	23	24	25
26	27	28	29	30	31	

April

Su	Mo	Tu	We	Th	Fr	Sa
						1
2	3	4	5	6	7	8
9	10	11	12	13	14	15
16	17	18	19	20	21	22
23	24	25	26	27	28	29
30						

May

Su	Mo	Tu	We	Th	Fr	Sa
	1	2	3	4	5	6
7	8	9	10	11	12	13
14	15	16	17	18	19	20
21	22	23	24	25	26	27
28	29	30	31			

June

Su	Mo	Tu	We	Th	Fr	Sa
				1	2	3
4	5	6	7	8	9	10
11	12	13	14	15	16	17
18	19	20	21	22	23	24
25	26	27	28	29	30	

July

Su	Mo	Tu	We	Th	Fr	Sa
						1
2	3	4	5	6	7	8
9	10	11	12	13	14	15
16	17	18	19	20	21	22
23	24	25	26	27	28	29
30	31					

August

Su	Mo	Tu	We	Th	Fr	Sa
		1	2	3	4	5
6	7	8	9	10	11	12
13	14	15	16	17	18	19
20	21	22	23	24	25	26
27	28	29	30	31		

September

Su	Mo	Tu	We	Th	Fr	Sa
					1	2
3	4	5	6	7	8	9
10	11	12	13	14	15	16
17	18	19	20	21	22	23
24	25	26	27	28	29	30

October

Su	Mo	Tu	We	Th	Fr	Sa
1	2	3	4	5	6	7
8	9	10	11	12	13	14
15	16	17	18	19	20	21
22	23	24	25	26	27	28
29	30	31				

November

Su	Mo	Tu	We	Th	Fr	Sa
			1	2	3	4
5	6	7	8	9	10	11
12	13	14	15	16	17	18
19	20	21	22	23	24	25
26	27	28	29	30		

December

Su	Mo	Tu	We	Th	Fr	Sa
					1	2
3	4	5	6	7	8	9
10	11	12	13	14	15	16
17	18	19	20	21	22	23
24	25	26	27	28	29	30
31						

2
0
2
3
.
.
.

"The artist must possess the courageous soul that dares and defies."
— Kate Chopin

JAN2023

SUN	MON	TUE	WED	THU	FRI	SAT
01	02	03	04	05	06	07
08	09	10	11	12	13	14
15	16	17	18	19	20	21
22	23	24	25	26	27	28
29	30	31				

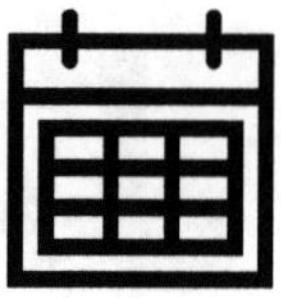

FEB2023

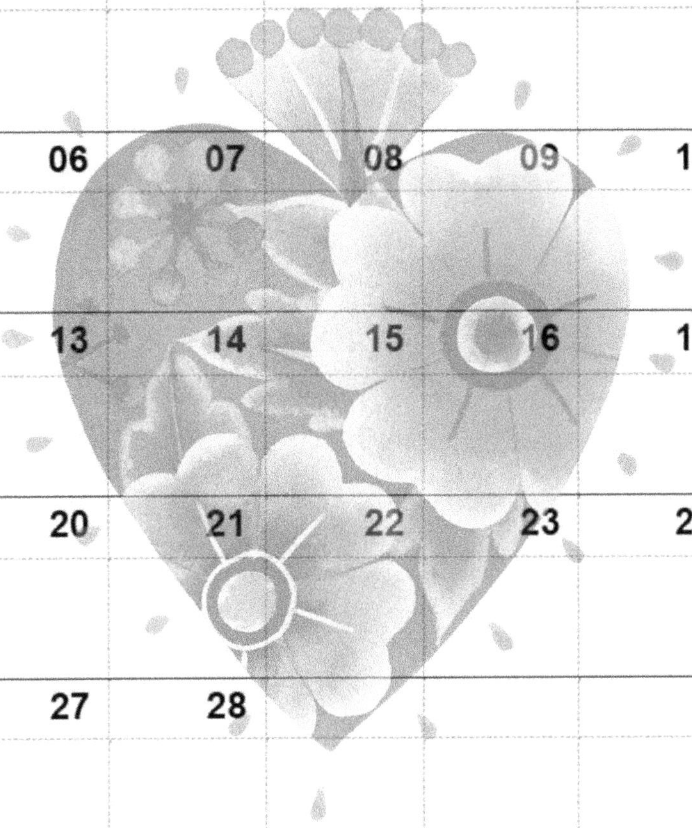

SUN	MON	TUE	WED	THU	FRI	SAT
			01	02	03	04
05	06	07	08	09	10	11
12	13	14	15	16	17	18
19	20	21	22	23	24	25
26	27	28				

MAR2023

SUN	MON	TUE	WED	THU	FRI	SAT
			01	02	03	04
05	06	07	08	09	10	11
12	13	14	15	16	17	18
19	20	21	22	23	24	25
26	27	28	29	30	31	

APR2023

SUN	MON	TUE	WED	THU	FRI	SAT
						01
02	03	04	05	06	07	08
09	10	11	12	13	14	15
16	17	18	19	20	21	22
23	24	25	26	27	28	29
30						

MAY2023

SUN	MON	TUE	WED	THU	FRI	SAT
	01	02	03	04	05	06
07	08	09	10	11	12	13
14	15	16	17	18	19	20
21	22	23	24	25	26	27
28	29	30	31			

JUN2023

SUN	MON	TUE	WED	THU	FRI	SAT
				01	02	03
04	05	06	07	08	09	10
11	12	13	14	15	16	17
18	19	20	21	22	23	24
25	26	27	28	29	30	

JUL2023

SUN	MON	TUE	WED	THU	FRI	SAT
						01
02	03	04	05	06	07	08
09	10	11	12	13	14	15
16	17	18	19	20	21	22
23	24	25	26	27	28	29
30	31					

AUG2023

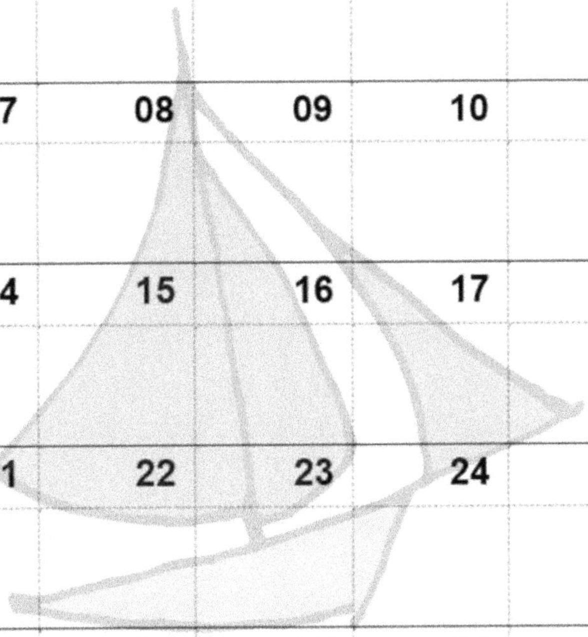

SUN	MON	TUE	WED	THU	FRI	SAT
		01	02	03	04	05
06	07	08	09	10	11	12
13	14	15	16	17	18	19
20	21	22	23	24	25	26
27	28	29	30	31		

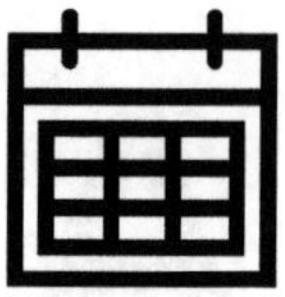

SEP2023

SUN	MON	TUE	WED	THU	FRI	SAT
					01	02
03	04	05	06	07	08	09
10	11	12	13	14	15	16
17	18	19	20	21	22	23
24	25	26	27	28	29	30

OCT2023

SUN	MON	TUE	WED	THU	FRI	SAT
01	02	03	04	05	06	07
08	09	10	11	12	13	14
15	16	17	18	19	20	21
22	23	24	25	26	27	28
29	30	31				

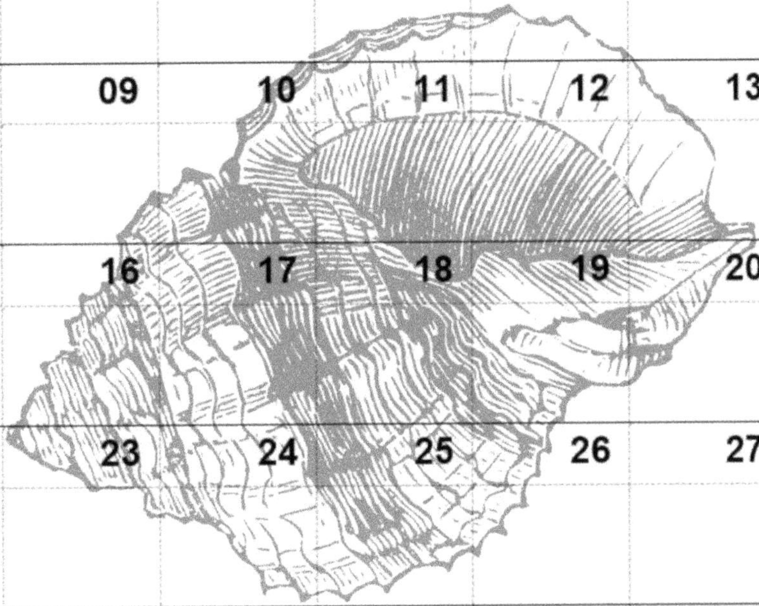

NOV2023

SUN	MON	TUE	WED	THU	FRI	SAT
			01	02	03	04
05	06	07	08	09	10	11
12	13	14	15	16	17	18
19	20	21	22	23	24	25
26	27	28	29	30		

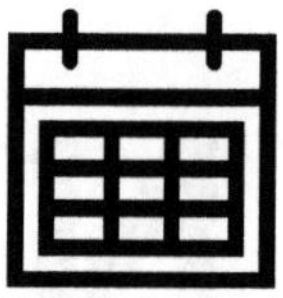

DEC2023

SUN	MON	TUE	WED	THU	FRI	SAT
					01	02
03	04	05	06	07	08	09
10	11	12	13	14	15	16
17	18	19	20	21	22	23
24	25	26	27	28	29	30
31						

2024

January

Su	Mo	Tu	We	Th	Fr	Sa
	1	2	3	4	5	6
7	8	9	10	11	12	13
14	15	16	17	18	19	20
21	22	23	24	25	26	27
28	29	30	31			

February

Su	Mo	Tu	We	Th	Fr	Sa
				1	2	3
4	5	6	7	8	9	10
11	12	13	14	15	16	17
18	19	20	21	22	23	24
25	26	27	28	29		

March

Su	Mo	Tu	We	Th	Fr	Sa
					1	2
3	4	5	6	7	8	9
10	11	12	13	14	15	16
17	18	19	20	21	22	23
24	25	26	27	28	29	30
31						

April

Su	Mo	Tu	We	Th	Fr	Sa
	1	2	3	4	5	6
7	8	9	10	11	12	13
14	15	16	17	18	19	20
21	22	23	24	25	26	27
28	29	30				

May

Su	Mo	Tu	We	Th	Fr	Sa
			1	2	3	4
5	6	7	8	9	10	11
12	13	14	15	16	17	18
19	20	21	22	23	24	25
26	27	28	29	30	31	

June

Su	Mo	Tu	We	Th	Fr	Sa
						1
2	3	4	5	6	7	8
9	10	11	12	13	14	15
16	17	18	19	20	21	22
23	24	25	26	27	28	29
30						

July

Su	Mo	Tu	We	Th	Fr	Sa
	1	2	3	4	5	6
7	8	9	10	11	12	13
14	15	16	17	18	19	20
21	22	23	24	25	26	27
28	29	30	31			

August

Su	Mo	Tu	We	Th	Fr	Sa
				1	2	3
4	5	6	7	8	9	10
11	12	13	14	15	16	17
18	19	20	21	22	23	24
25	26	27	28	29	30	31

September

Su	Mo	Tu	We	Th	Fr	Sa
1	2	3	4	5	6	7
8	9	10	11	12	13	14
15	16	17	18	19	20	21
22	23	24	25	26	27	28
29	30					

October

Su	Mo	Tu	We	Th	Fr	Sa
		1	2	3	4	5
6	7	8	9	10	11	12
13	14	15	16	17	18	19
20	21	22	23	24	25	26
27	28	29	30	31		

November

Su	Mo	Tu	We	Th	Fr	Sa
					1	2
3	4	5	6	7	8	9
10	11	12	13	14	15	16
17	18	19	20	21	22	23
24	25	26	27	28	29	30

December

Su	Mo	Tu	We	Th	Fr	Sa
1	2	3	4	5	6	7
8	9	10	11	12	13	14
15	16	17	18	19	20	21
22	23	24	25	26	27	28
29	30	31				

2
0
2
4
.
.
.

JAN2024

SUN	MON	TUE	WED	THU	FRI	SAT
	01	02	03	04	05	06
07	08	09	10	11	12	13
14	15	16	17	18	19	20
21	22	23	24	25	26	27
28	29	30	31			

"In books I have traveled, not only to other worlds, but into my own."
— Anna Quindlen

And now, write your own world...

BE
CREATIVE
BRAINSTORM
IDEA
BE
CREATIVE

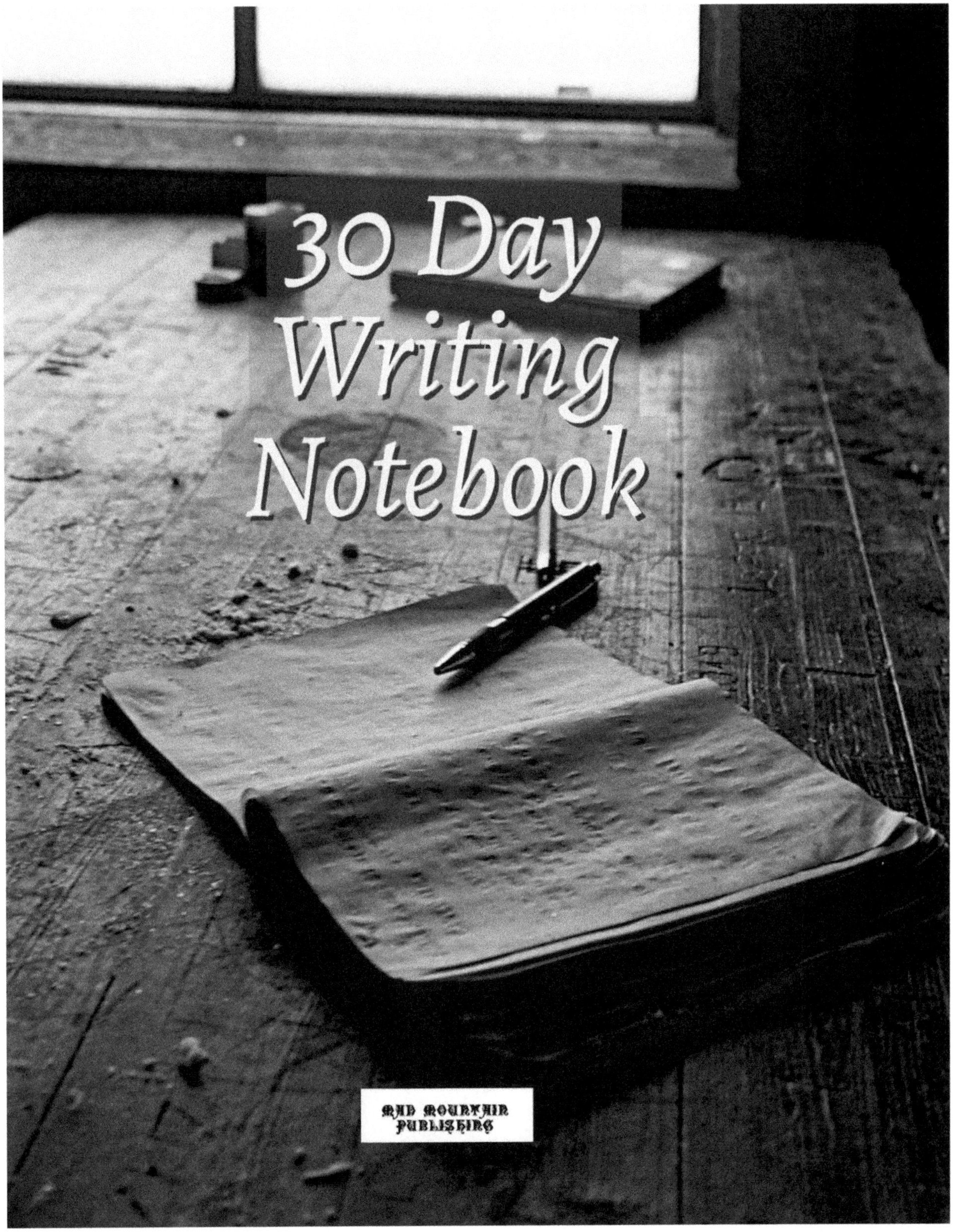
30 Day
Writing
Notebook
MAD MOUNTAIN
PUBLISHING

Take 30 days and write your novel!
Get your first draft on paper in 30 days with this Notebook...

This is a basic Notebook designed especially for those who want to write their novels in 30-Day time periods. You can set your own pace: your writing days do not have to be consecutive, but you should aim to complete one day's work within 24 hours. Think of it as 'sectional' or 'segmented' writing: there is a beginning, middle and end to your daily output. For many writers, this can work to prevent 'writer's block', wherein you have an idea, but it doesn't necessarily 'fit' where you are at the moment in your draft, but you go ahead and write that segment; moving it later, in your second or third draft .. The point is to get it all down for editing later.

Divided into Week 1 through Week 4, each section contains 7 days with 8 pages (37 narrow lines to a page) to write on for each day. The 29th and 30th days follow Week 4. Each page is designed with a 1-inch margin on the left, a Word Count box at the bottom, and extra white space for additional notes and/or color/sticky note highlights. A Planning Page is placed at the start of each week. Three additional pages for Notes are appended at the end.

Tips for *success...*
1) Create a writing sanctuary, a space all your own where you can return each day to write.

2) Try to schedule your writing time to minimize interruptions.

3) Keep dictionary/thesaurus, the books of authors who inspire you, your totems, etc., within reach while you write.

4) Check Twitter, Facebook, Instagram, etc., before beginning to write each day (and as soon as you finish, if you find that rewarding).

5) If you miss a day writing, simply return to it when you can: the 30 Days do not have to be consecutive. It is more important in the long run to continue writing, to tell your story, get it down on paper and in a concise, easily editable format. Once you finish this Notebook, go to your computer and begin typing from it: you will find yourself immediately back in your story and will readily see just where you need to start your editing.

WEEK 1

DAY 1

WORD COUNT:

DAY 1

WORD COUNT:

DAY 1

WORD COUNT:

DAY 1

WORD COUNT:

DAY 1

WORD COUNT:

DAY 1

WORD COUNT:

DAY 1

WORD COUNT:

DAY 1

WORD COUNT:

DAY 2

WORD COUNT:

DAY 2

WORD COUNT:

DAY 2

WORD COUNT:

DAY 2

WORD COUNT:

DAY 2

WORD COUNT:

DAY 2

WORD COUNT:

DAY 2

WORD COUNT:

DAY 2

WORD COUNT:

DAY 3

WORD COUNT:

DAY 3

WORD COUNT:

DAY 3

WORD COUNT:

DAY 3

WORD COUNT:

DAY 3

WORD COUNT:

DAY 3

WORD COUNT:

DAY 3

WORD COUNT:

DAY 3

WORD COUNT:

DAY 4

WORD COUNT:

DAY 4

WORD COUNT:

DAY 4

WORD COUNT:

DAY 4

WORD COUNT:

DAY 4

WORD COUNT:

DAY 4

WORD COUNT:

DAY 4

WORD COUNT:

DAY 4

WORD COUNT:

DAY 5

WORD COUNT:

DAY 5

WORD COUNT:

DAY 5

WORD COUNT:

DAY 5

WORD COUNT:

DAY 5

WORD COUNT:

DAY 5

WORD COUNT:

DAY 5

WORD COUNT:

DAY 5

WORD COUNT:

DAY 6

WORD COUNT:

DAY 6

WORD COUNT:

DAY 6

WORD COUNT:

DAY 6

WORD COUNT:

DAY 6

WORD COUNT:

DAY 6

WORD COUNT:

DAY 6

WORD COUNT:

DAY 6

WORD COUNT:

DAY 7

WORD COUNT:

DAY 7

WORD COUNT:

DAY 7

WORD COUNT:

DAY 7

WORD COUNT:

DAY 7

WORD COUNT:

DAY 7

WORD COUNT:

DAY 7

WORD COUNT:

DAY 7

WORD COUNT:

WEEK 2

DAY 8

WORD COUNT:

DAY 8

WORD COUNT:

DAY 8

WORD COUNT:

DAY 8

WORD COUNT:

DAY 8

WORD COUNT:

DAY 8

WORD COUNT:

DAY 8

WORD COUNT:

DAY 8

WORD COUNT:

DAY 9

WORD COUNT:

DAY 9

WORD COUNT:

DAY 9

WORD COUNT:

DAY 9

WORD COUNT:

DAY 9

WORD COUNT:

DAY 9

WORD COUNT:

DAY 9

WORD COUNT:

DAY 9

WORD COUNT:

DAY 10

WORD COUNT:

DAY 10

WORD COUNT:

DAY 10

WORD COUNT:

DAY 10

WORD COUNT:

DAY 10

WORD COUNT:

DAY 10

WORD COUNT:

DAY 10

WORD COUNT:

DAY 10

WORD COUNT:

DAY 11

WORD COUNT:

DAY 11

WORD COUNT:

DAY 11

WORD COUNT:

DAY 11

WORD COUNT:

DAY 11

WORD COUNT:

DAY 11

WORD COUNT:

DAY 11

WORD COUNT:

DAY 11

WORD COUNT:

DAY 12

WORD COUNT:

DAY 12

WORD COUNT:

DAY 12

WORD COUNT:

DAY 12

WORD COUNT:

DAY 12

WORD COUNT:

DAY 12

WORD COUNT:

DAY 12

WORD COUNT:

DAY 12

WORD COUNT:

DAY 13

WORD COUNT:

DAY 13

WORD COUNT:

DAY 13

WORD COUNT:

DAY 13

WORD COUNT:

DAY 13

WORD COUNT:

DAY 13

WORD COUNT:

DAY 13

WORD COUNT:

DAY 13

WORD COUNT:

DAY 14

WORD COUNT:

DAY 14

WORD COUNT:

DAY 14

WORD COUNT:

DAY 14

WORD COUNT:

DAY 14

WORD COUNT:

DAY 14

WORD COUNT:

DAY 14

WORD COUNT:

DAY 14

WORD COUNT:

WEEK 3

DAY 15

WORD COUNT:

DAY 15

WORD COUNT:

DAY 15

WORD COUNT:

DAY 15

WORD COUNT:

DAY 15

WORD COUNT:

DAY 15

WORD COUNT:

DAY 15

WORD COUNT:

DAY 15

WORD COUNT:

DAY 16

WORD COUNT:

DAY 16

WORD COUNT:

DAY 16

WORD COUNT:

DAY 16

WORD COUNT:

DAY 16

WORD COUNT:

DAY 16

WORD COUNT:

DAY 16

WORD COUNT:

DAY 16

WORD COUNT:

DAY 17

WORD COUNT:

DAY 17

WORD COUNT:

DAY 17

WORD COUNT:

DAY 17

WORD COUNT:

DAY 17

WORD COUNT:

DAY 17

WORD COUNT:

DAY 17

WORD COUNT:

DAY 17

WORD COUNT:

DAY 18

WORD COUNT:

DAY 18

WORD COUNT:

DAY 18

WORD COUNT:

DAY 18

WORD COUNT:

DAY 18

WORD COUNT:

DAY 18

WORD COUNT:

DAY 18

WORD COUNT:

DAY 18

WORD COUNT:

DAY 19

WORD COUNT:

DAY 19

WORD COUNT:

DAY 19

WORD COUNT:

DAY 19

WORD COUNT:

DAY 19

WORD COUNT:

DAY 19

WORD COUNT:

DAY 19

WORD COUNT:

DAY 19

WORD COUNT:

DAY 20

WORD COUNT:

DAY 20

WORD COUNT:

WORD COUNT:

DAY 20

WORD COUNT:

DAY 20

WORD COUNT:

DAY 20

WORD COUNT:

DAY 20

WORD COUNT:

DAY 20

WORD COUNT:

DAY 21

WORD COUNT:

DAY 21

WORD COUNT:

DAY 21

WORD COUNT:

DAY 21

WORD COUNT:

DAY 21

WORD COUNT:

DAY 21

WORD COUNT:

DAY 21

WORD COUNT:

DAY 21

WORD COUNT:

WEEK 4

DAY 22

WORD COUNT:

DAY 22

WORD COUNT:

DAY 22

WORD COUNT:

DAY 22

WORD COUNT:

DAY 22

WORD COUNT:

DAY 22

WORD COUNT:

DAY 22

WORD COUNT:

DAY 22

WORD COUNT:

DAY 23

WORD COUNT:

DAY 23

WORD COUNT:

DAY 23

WORD COUNT:

DAY 23

DAY 23

WORD COUNT:

DAY 23

WORD COUNT:

DAY 23

WORD COUNT:

DAY 23

WORD COUNT:

DAY 24

WORD COUNT:

DAY 24

WORD COUNT:

DAY 24

WORD COUNT:

DAY 24

WORD COUNT:

DAY 24

WORD COUNT:

DAY 24

WORD COUNT:

DAY 24

WORD COUNT:

DAY 24

WORD COUNT:

DAY 25

WORD COUNT:

DAY 25

WORD COUNT:

DAY 25

WORD COUNT:

DAY 25

WORD COUNT:

DAY 25

WORD COUNT:

DAY 25

WORD COUNT:

DAY 25

WORD COUNT:

DAY 25

WORD COUNT:

DAY 26

WORD COUNT:

DAY 26

WORD COUNT:

DAY 26

WORD COUNT:

DAY 26

WORD COUNT:

DAY 26

WORD COUNT:

DAY 26

WORD COUNT:

DAY 26

WORD COUNT:

DAY 26

WORD COUNT:

DAY 27

WORD COUNT:

DAY 27

WORD COUNT:

DAY 27

WORD COUNT:

DAY 27

WORD COUNT:

DAY 27

WORD COUNT:

DAY 27

WORD COUNT:

DAY 27

WORD COUNT:

DAY 27

WORD COUNT:

DAY 28

WORD COUNT:

DAY 28

WORD COUNT:

DAY 28

WORD COUNT:

DAY 28

WORD COUNT:

DAY 28

WORD COUNT:

DAY 28

WORD COUNT:

DAY 28

WORD COUNT:

DAY 28

WORD COUNT:

TWO MORE DAYS...

DAY 29

WORD COUNT:

DAY 29

WORD COUNT:

DAY 29

WORD COUNT:

DAY 29

WORD COUNT:

DAY 29

WORD COUNT:

DAY 29

WORD COUNT:

DAY 29

WORD COUNT:

DAY 29

WORD COUNT:

DAY 30

WORD COUNT:

DAY 30

WORD COUNT:

DAY 30

WORD COUNT:

DAY 30

WORD COUNT:

DAY 30

WORD COUNT:

DAY 30

WORD COUNT:

DAY 30

WORD COUNT:

DAY 30

WORD COUNT:

NOTES

Current Titles Available Worldwide
Irish Heath and Bog
30 Day Writing Notebook
(Amber Raven Edition)
1,000 Quotes For Writers
(eBook & Print)
Order our books via online book retailers or ask for
them by title from your local bookseller!

CPSIA information can be obtained
at www.ICGtesting.com
Printed in the USA
LVHW061201130422
716028LV00011B/509

9 780578 360775